Tiny Talks

Volume 1 – Temples

**A year's worth of simple messages
that can be given during Primary
or Family Home Evening**

Volume 1–Temples

**A year's worth of simple messages
that can be given during Primary
or Family Home Evening**

By Tammy & Chad Daybell

Illustrated by Adam Ford

CFI

Springville, Utah

ISBN: 1-55517-612-7
v.1

Published by CFI
Imprint of Cedar Fort Inc.
www.cedarfort.com

Distributed by:

Cover design and illustrations by Adam Ford
Cover design © 2002 by Lyle Mortimer
Illustrations © 2002 by Adam Ford

Printed in the United States of America
10 9 8 7 6 5 4 3 2 1

Printed on acid-free paper

Table of Contents

Introduction

As the parents of five young children, we have experienced the challenge of writing a Primary talk that is simple enough for our child to read, as well as have it be interesting to the children in the audience. To help other parents in our situation, we have compiled dozens of these presentations into one handy volume.

It is our desire that the next time your six-year-old child says, "Mom, I have to give a talk in Primary today," you'll be able to tie everyone's shoes, comb their hair, get to church on time, and still have your child give a meaningful talk!

These talks can be used in many ways. If a talk is used in Primary, we suggest the child give the talk while holding up the picture at the appropriate time. The child could conclude with a short testimony about the topic, and close by saying, "In the name of Jesus Christ, amen."

We have found that visual aids greatly enhance a talk. With each talk we have listed pictures that could be used from the Gospel Art Picture Kit (GAPK). It is available from the Church Distribution Center. If you don't have one, your meetinghouse library might have a set. The meetinghouse library may also have other pictures available that fit the talk.

Within some of the talks you will find small footnote numbers. These correspond to the list of sources at the end of the book.

Tammy and Chad Daybell

Chapter 1

I love to see the temple

A temple is a special place

Scripture:

Who shall stand in his holy place? He that hath clean hands, and a pure heart.
(Psalms 24:3-4)

Heavenly Father has always commanded his people to build temples. A temple is a special place where we learn more about Heavenly Father and Jesus. In the temple we perform sacred ordinances, such as baptisms for those who have died. Marriages are also performed there, so families can live together forever.

To enter the temple, you will first have an interview with the bishop, and he will ask whether you are keeping the commandments, and trying to do what is right. When we keep the commandments, we are happier and have a desire to help other people. This also makes us worthy to live again with Heavenly Father.

The Kirtland Temple

The Kirtland Temple was the first temple built by the Church of Jesus Christ of Latter-day Saints. It is in the state of Ohio. The church members worked very hard for more than three years to finish it.

The Prophet Joseph Smith saw the building's pattern in a heavenly vision before it was built. He then described the temple to the church architect, who drew the plans just as the prophet had described it. [1]

The church members had many spiritual experiences and heavenly visions in the Kirtland Temple, including visits from the ancient prophets Moses and Elijah, and from the Savior himself.

Scripture:

And that this house may be a house of prayer, a house of fasting, a house of faith, a house of glory and of God.
(D&C 109:16)

Visual Aid:
GAPK #500 Kirtland Temple

3

Scripture:

And we are willing to enter into a covenant with our God to do his will, and to be obedient to his commandments in all things that he shall command us, all the remainder of our days, that we may not bring upon ourselves a never-ending torment, as has been spoken by the angel, that we may not drink out of the cup of the wrath of God.
(Mosiah 5:5)

Visual Aid:
GAPK #307 King Benjamin addresses his people

King Benjamin's people gathered at the temple

King Benjamin was one of the greatest leaders in the Book of Mormon. He was a righteous king, and his people followed Heavenly Father's commandments. King Benjamin became very old, but he wanted to speak to his people one more time before he died. He asked his whole kingdom to come to their temple in Zarahemla.

When all of the people had gathered around the temple, he taught them the importance of obeying the commandments and serving one another. The people promised to obey Heavenly Father. King Benjamin said when we serve other people by doing kind deeds, we make Heavenly Father happy. The teachings of King Benjamin are still true today.

Reading the Bible by coal-oil light

When President Spencer W. Kimball was a boy, he heard a church leader speak on the importance of reading the scriptures. That very night young Spencer went home, climbed up to his room in the attic, lighted a little coal-oil lamp, and then started reading the Bible.

He read in the Bible every night. He later said, "A year later I closed the Bible, having read every chapter in that big and glorious book. . . . Now I am not telling you this story to boast; I am merely using this as an example to say that if I could do it by coal-oil light, you can do it by electric light. I have always been glad I read the Bible cover to cover."[2]

If we read the scriptures each night, we will learn right from wrong and we will receive blessings from Heavenly Father.

Scripture:

O, remember, my son, and learn wisdom in thy youth; yea, learn in thy youth to keep the commandments of God.
(Alma 37:35)

Visual Aids:
GAPK #517
Spencer W. Kimball

GAPK #617
Girl reading the Scriptures

Chapter 2

My family can be together forever

Elijah restored the sealing power

Scripture:

And I will give unto thee the keys of the kingdom of heaven: and whatsoever thou shalt bind on earth shall be bound in heaven. (Matthew 16:19)

When Jesus was on the earth, he gave the priesthood power to his apostles. The leaders of his church were Peter, James and John. But after many years, the people turned wicked and killed the apostles. The priesthood power was taken from the earth for many years. But Heavenly Father sent Peter, James and John as resurrected beings to restore the priesthood to Joseph Smith.

Later, Joseph also received the sealing power of the priesthood from the prophet Elijah in the Kirtland Temple. This sealing power is used today in the temples to seal families together forever. When a family is sealed together and lives righteously, they will someday live with Heavenly Father in the Celestial Kingdom.

Visual Aids:

GAPK # 408
Melchizedek Priesthood
is restored

GAPK # 417
Elijah restores the power
to seal families for eternity

Marriages should last for eternity

When Joseph Smith was a boy, the true church was not on the earth. But Heavenly Father and Jesus appeared to Joseph, and told him he would be called as a prophet to restore The Church of Jesus Christ to the earth. Joseph received many revelations, including several that show the importance of being married in the temple.

Today, when people get married somewhere other than in the temple, the minister often says, "I pronounce you husband and wife until death do you part." This means that when these people die, they won't be husband and wife anymore, because they weren't married in the temple. But during a temple marriage, a couple is promised that if they live righteously, they will be together with their family forever. When a family is sealed together and lives righteously, they will someday live with Heavenly Father in the Celestial Kingdom.

Scripture:

And again, I say unto you, if a man marry a wife by my word, which is my law, and by the new and everlasting covenant, and it is sealed unto them by the Holy Spirit of promise, by him who is anointed, unto whom I have appointed this power and the keys of the priesthood; and it shall be said unto them—Ye shall come forth in the first resurrection. (D&C 132:19)

Visual Aids:
GAPK # 403 The First Vision

GAPK #609 Newly married couple in front of the temple

9

Enoch trusted the Lord

Scripture:

And verily, verily I say unto you, that whatsoever you seal on earth shall be sealed in heaven; and whatsoever you bind on earth, in my name and my word, saith the Lord, it shall be eternally bound in the heavens.
(D&C 132:46)

Visual Aid:
GAPK #120
Enoch and his people are taken up to heaven

Long before the Noah's Flood lived a young boy named Enoch. He was shy and humble, and often had trouble talking. Other people would make fun of him. But one day he heard Heavenly Father's voice calling him to be a prophet. Enoch was very surprised. He knelt on the ground, and asked the Lord, "Why me? All the people hate me because I speak slowly."

But Heavenly Father told Enoch that if he would preach the gospel he would be blessed. And that is what happened. Enoch obeyed Heavenly Father and became a powerful teacher. Many people believed his teachings, and they built a great city. Heavenly Father also gave Enoch the sealing power, and Enoch's people built temples and became a righteous people. They became so righteous that Heavenly Father took their whole city to Heaven.

Joseph Smith saw the Celestial Kingdom

The Prophet Joseph Smith had a special older brother named Alvin. Joseph loved Alvin very much. But one day Alvin became very sick, and he died. His death made Joseph feel sad, because the true church hadn't been restored yet. Joseph was worried that Alvin wouldn't make it into heaven.

But a few years later Joseph received a vision of the Celestial Kingdom, and he saw that his brother Alvin was there! Joseph was very happy, and he asked Heavenly Father how Alvin could be there, since he had never been baptized. Heavenly Father told Joseph that people who died without hearing the gospel, who would have accepted it, can live in the Celestial Kingdom if we do their temple work.[3] Joseph made sure Alvin's temple work was done. If we do our ancestors' temple work, they can accept the gospel and live in the Celestial Kingdom, too.

Scripture:

For I am the Lord thy God, and will be with thee even unto the end of the world, and through all eternity; for verily I seal upon you your exaltation, and prepare a throne for you in the kingdom of my Father. (D&C 132:49)

Visual Aid:
GAPK #504
Temple baptismal font

GAPK #400 Joseph Smith

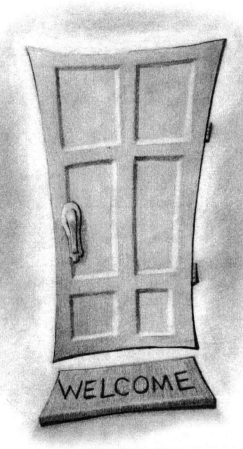

Chapter 3

The temple is the house of the Lord

Jesus cleansed Jerusalem's temple

Scripture:

And early in the morning he came again into the temple, and all the people came unto him; and he sat down and taught them.
(John 8:2)

Jesus loved to go to the temple in Jerusalem. He knew it was a holy place. One time he went to the temple to teach the gospel, but there were many people in the temple who were making noise. These people weren't being reverent. They were trying to sell things and weren't treating the temple with respect. This made Jesus angry, and he made them all leave the temple. He told them, "This is a house of prayer." The wicked people knew they had been acting wrong, and they left.

We should always treat temples and church buildings with respect and reverence. We should help keep them clean and looking their best, because they are sacred places where we learn about Heavenly Father.

Visual Aid:
GAPK #224
Jesus cleansing the temple

The Savior visited the Kirtland Temple

The members of the Church worked very hard for three years to build the Kirtland Temple. Heavenly Father and Jesus were very pleased with the church members. A few days after the temple was finished, Jesus visited Joseph Smith and Oliver Cowdery inside the temple. Jesus told them he had accepted the temple, and that they could be happy with the work they had done.

Jesus is always happy when new temples are built. Temples are very special places where we learn more about the gospel plan and perform ordinances for our ancestors who have died. When we do temple work, we are helping people in the spirit world be able to live with Heavenly Father.

Scripture:

We saw the Lord standing upon the breastwork of the pulpit, before us; and under his feet was a paved work of pure gold, in color like amber, His eyes were as a flame of fire; the hair of his head was white like the pure snow; his countenance shone above the brightness of the sun; and his voice was as the sound of the rushing of great waters.
(D&C 110:2-3)

Visual Aid:
GAPK#500 Kirtland Temple

Lorenzo Snow talked with Jesus

Scripture:

Yea, and my presence shall be there, for I will come unto it, and all the pure in heart that shall come into it shall see God. (D&C 97:16)

Lorenzo Snow was the fifth president of the church. Soon after becoming the prophet, he was walking down a hall in the Salt Lake Temple when Jesus Christ appeared to him. President Snow later told this story to his granddaughter Allie when they were in the temple together. He took her to the spot where Jesus had visited him and told her, "He stood right here, about three feet above the floor. It looked as though he stood on a plate of solid gold."

President Snow then told his granddaughter what a glorious person the Savior is. Finally he told her, "Now granddaughter, I want you to remember that this is the testimony of your grandfather, that he told you with his own lips that he actually saw the Savior, here in the temple, and talked with him face to face."[4]

Visual Aid:
GAPK #510 Lorenzo Snow

The Saints sacrificed to build a temple

When the church first began, the members were often made fun of for believing the gospel. Sometimes wicked men would even try to kill them. It got so bad that all the members had to leave their homes, and they moved to a new city called Nauvoo in the state of Illinois. Soon after they arrived, the Lord commanded them to build a temple.

This was a very hard commandment for the church members to obey, because they didn't have any money. Some people didn't even have houses or enough food to eat. But everyone helped each other, and they slowly built the temple. Within a few years they had built the Nauvoo Temple on a hill above the Mississippi River. Many of the Relief Society women collected pennies so they could buy curtains for the temple. The Saints had sacrificed much, but they were very blessed by the Lord.

Scripture:

For thou knowest that we have done this work through great tribulation; and out of our poverty we have given of our substance to build a house to thy name, that the Son of Man might have a place to manifest himself to his people.
(D&C 109:5)

Visual Aid:
GAPK # 501
Nauvoo Temple

Chapter 4

The temple brings the blessings of heaven to earth

Satan doesn't like temple work

Scripture:

And, if you keep my commandments and endure to the end you shall have eternal life, which gift is the greatest of all the gifts of God.
(D&C 14:7)

Visual Aid:
GAPK #240
The Resurrected Savior

(Picture of Logan Temple not available in Gospel Art kit)

The Savior has said that temple work is one of the most important things we can do. Satan doesn't want us to do temple work. One day, Logan Temple president Marriner F. Merrill saw a group of people coming toward the temple. They stopped near the temple, and soon their leader came into President Merrill's office.

"Who are you?" President Merrill asked. The man said, "I am Satan, and these are my followers. I don't like the work you are doing in this temple. Will you stop it?" President Merrill said, "No, I will not stop it!"

Satan then told him, "If you will not stop it, I will have my followers whisper in the ears of the people to not go to the temple." Satan then left.

President Merrill said the temple work did slow down, and only when the people realized Satan was working on them did they become more faithful and begin attending the temple again.[5]

Temples are built through revelation

When the Nauvoo Temple was being planned, Elder William Weeks was called to be the architect. He designed some plans, and showed them to the Prophet Joseph Smith. The plans didn't include large circular windows that Joseph had asked for. Joseph told Brother Weeks the temple had to have the circular windows. Joseph told him, "I have seen in vision the splendid appearance of the building, and will have it built according to the pattern shown me." Brother Weeks changed the design, and the circular windows worked out perfectly.[6]

The Lord can direct his prophets at any time. Just a few years ago, President Gordon B. Hinckley was traveling by car from a meeting in Mexico when he received inspiration on how to design a smaller temple that could be easily built for less cost. He sketched it out and later gave the plan to the temple architect. That temple design has now been used in dozens of temples across the world.[7]

Scripture:

Verily I say unto you, that it is my will that a house should be built unto me in the land of Zion, like unto the pattern which I have given you. Yea, let it be built speedily, by the tithing of my people. (D&C 97:10-11)

Visual Aids:
GAPK #501
Nauvoo Temple

GAPK #520
Gordon B. Hinckley

Scripture:

And inasmuch as my people build a house unto me in the name of the Lord, and do not suffer any unclean thing to come into it, that it be not defiled, my glory shall rest upon it. (D&C 97:15)

Visual Aids:

GAPK #502
Salt Lake Temple
GAPK # 507
Brigham Young

When the Pioneers arrived in the Salt Lake Valley in the year 1847, one of the first things the prophet Brigham Young did was choose a place to build the temple. But the Pioneers had many things to do first, such as build their own houses, and raise crops. They finally started building the Salt Lake Temple in 1853. But it was hard work. They had to cut the granite stone for the temple out of the mountain, and then bring it nearly twenty miles by wagon. The temple was finally dedicated in 1893. It took the church members forty years to complete the temple!

Their hard work paid off. The Salt Lake Temple is now one of the most well-known buildings in the world, and is a symbol of The Church of Jesus Christ of Latter-day Saints.

A beautiful sign of happiness

The temple is a place where special events often happen. Angels often come to the temples, and sometimes visitors have seen heavenly visions.

One night in 1886, the Logan Temple was flooded with a beautiful light that could be seen across the entire valley. This was before electric lights were available, and no one could explain what had happened. The same brilliant light returned the next night, lighting up the temple from top to bottom. Everyone knew something special was happening, and the temple president contacted President Wilford Woodruff about it. President Woodruff said the light was a sign of happiness from members of a large family who had been released from spirit prison because of the temple work that had been done for them in the Logan Temple.[8]

Scripture:

The Spirit itself beareth witness with our spirit, that we are the children of God. And if our children, then heirs; heirs of God and joint-heirs with Christ; if so be that we suffer with him, that we may be also glorified together. (Romans 8:16-17)

Visual Aid:
GAPK #509
Wilford Woodruff

(Picture of Logan Temple not available in Gospel Art kit)

Chapter 5

My body
is a temple

Scripture:

Know ye not that ye are the temple of God, and that the Spirit of God dwelleth in you? . . . For the temple of God is holy, which temple ye are.
(1 Corinthians 3:16-17)

Visual Aid:
GAPK #608
Jesus surrounded by modern-day children

Our bodies are special gifts from Heavenly Father. They are more amazing than any machine, and our brains work faster than a computer. The scriptures say our bodies are like temples, and Jesus is happy when we keep them free from sin and evil. Our body is the house of our spirit, and we should keep it as clean as we would keep the temple. Smoking cigarettes, drinking beer or taking drugs only hurts our bodies.

If we keep our bodies and minds clean, the Holy Ghost will tell us the right things to do. The Holy Ghost won't visit people who act wickedly. We should try to do what is right so the Holy Ghost will help us make correct choices.

Swear not at all

Long ago, when Moses was the prophet, the Lord commanded him to climb to the top of a high mountain. While Moses was standing on the mountain the Lord gave him the Ten Commandments. One of the commandments says we should never take the Lord's name in vain.

Church leaders also say we shouldn't swear, use dirty words, or tell naughty jokes. At school sometimes we hear bad language. But even though some people think saying bad words is okay, it is wrong. President Hinckley has said we can be an example to others by not swearing.

Satan wants everyone to use bad words, but Jesus said, "Swear not at all." When we choose to only use kind words, it makes Heavenly Father very happy.

Scripture:

Thou shalt not take the name of the Lord thy God in vain; for the Lord will not hold him guiltless that taketh his name in vain. (Exodus 20:7)

Visual Aid:
GAPK #520
Gordon B. Hinckley

Daniel obeyed Heavenly Father

Scripture:

As for these four children, God gave them knowledge and skill in all learning and wisdom: and Daniel had understanding in all visions and dreams. (Daniel 1:17)

The prophet Daniel lived many centuries ago. When he was a young man, he was taken captive by the king of Babylon. The king tried to make Daniel and his friends drink wine and eat food that wasn't good for them. They refused, because they knew Heavenly Father wouldn't be happy. Instead, they asked for good food and water. The king soon noticed Daniel and his friends were healthier and wiser than the other children.

Heavenly Father has given us the Word of Wisdom to help us have strong bodies and minds. To be worthy to enter the temple, we must choose to live the Word of Wisdom. When we do, we will be blessed in many ways.

Visual Aid:
GAPK #114
Daniel refusing the
King's food and wine

Obeying the Word of Wisdom brings blessings

When Joseph Smith first restored the church, he would hold meetings with other church leaders. Many of the men would smoke pipes or cigars, or chew tobacco. By the end of the meeting, the room would be filled with smoke, and the floor would be sticky. Joseph's wife Emma would have to clean up the mess after each meeting.

Joseph asked Heavenly Father if this was right, and he received a revelation called the Word of Wisdom. It says we shouldn't smoke, or drink coffee, tea or alcohol. It also said that there are many good things to eat. Heavenly Father promises that both our bodies and minds will be blessed if we obey the Word of Wisdom.

Scripture:

And all saints who remember to keep and do all these sayings, walking in obedience to the commandments, shall receive health in their navel and marrow in their bones; And shall find wisdom and great treasures of knowledge, even hidden treasures. (D&C 89:18-19)

Visual Aid:
GAPK #401
Joseph Smith

GAPK #405
Emma Smith

Chapter 6

Temples are
a sign of
the true church

The Nauvoo Temple stands again

Scripture:

I command you, all ye my saints, to build a house unto me.
(D&C 124:31)

The original Nauvoo Temple was only used for a short time. It took several years of sacrifice and struggle by the church members to build it. Then right after it was completed, wicked men made the church members leave the city. In 1848 the temple caught fire, and soon only the bare walls were standing.

But it had been worth the effort to build it. After its dedication, thousands of Saints were able to do their temple work. The Nauvoo Temple was the first one with a baptismal font, and many baptisms for the dead took place there. Now the temple has been rebuilt in the same place, and is a wonderful reminder of the sacrifices made by the early church members.

Visual Aid:
GAPK #501
Nauvoo Temple

Heavenly Father's people always build temples

Heavenly Father has always commanded his people to have a special place to worship him. When Moses and the Israelites were in the wilderness, the Lord commanded Moses to build a tabernacle, which was like a temple. The tabernacle was a tent that could be folded up and carried when the people moved.

Later, the Lord commanded King David to build a temple in Jerusalem. He did build one, and his son Solomon later made the temple even bigger. Although many years have passed, parts of that temple still remain in Jerusalem. Now our church members obey Heavenly Father by building temples all over the world.

Scripture:

And Moses took the tabernacle, and pitched it without the camp, afar off from the camp. . . . As Moses entered into the tabernacle, the cloudy pillar descended, and stood at the door of the tabernacle, and the Lord talked with Moses.
(Exodus 33:7-9)

Visual Aid:
GAPK #118
Solomon's Temple

Nephi built a temple

And I, Nephi, did build a temple; and I did construct it after the manner of the temple of Solomon save it were not built of so many precious things; for they were not to be found upon the land, wherefore, it could not be built like unto Solomon's temple. But the manner of the construction was like unto the temple of Solomon; and the workmanship thereof was exceedingly fine.
(2 Nephi 5:16)

Visual Aids:
GAPK #302
Nephi and Lehi
GAPK # 500
Kirtland Temple

When Nephi arrived in the promised land, the Lord commanded him to build a temple. As a boy growing up in Jerusalem, Nephi had seen Solomon's temple and he built his temple just like it. The Nephites did their very best work on the temple.

When the Saints built the Kirtland Temple, the women broke up their finest china dishes to mix into the materials for the outside walls. Their broken dishes made the temple sparkle in the sunlight.

Today our church does all it can to make our temples as nice as possible. We build them with the finest materials. We want each temple to be beautiful, because it is the House of the Lord.

Prophets choose temple sites

The Lord has always inspired his prophets where to build temples. For example, when the city of St. George, Utah, was first settled, the prophet Brigham Young visited the people there. Many of the citizens wanted to build a temple on top of a sandstone cliff, but the prophet drove his wagon to the lowest point in the valley, which was a swamp.

President Young explained that the temple must be built there, because the Nephites had once dedicated that very spot for a temple, but they had never completed it. It took months for the Saints to drain the swamp, but the temple was built, and now stands in the center of the city of St. George.[9]

Scripture:

And verily, I say unto you, let this house be built unto my name, that I may reveal mine ordinances therein unto my people. . . And ye shall build it on the place where you have contemplated building it, for that is the spot which I have chosen for you to build it.
(D&C 124:40-43)

Visual Aid:
GAPK #507
Brigham Young

Chapter 7

Temples bless children throughout the world

Baby Jesus at the temple

Scripture:

There was a man in Jerusalem, whose name was Simeon. . . And he came by the Spirit into the temple; and when the parents brought in the child Jesus . . . he took him up in his arms, and blessed God, and said, Lord, now lettest thou thy servant depart in peace . . . For mine eyes have seen thy salvation. (Luke 2:25-30)

Visual Aid:
GAPK # 201
Baby Jesus

When Jesus was just a baby, Mary and Joseph took him to the temple in Jerusalem. While they were there, an old man named Simeon saw them. Simeon had been righteous all his life, and Heavenly Father had promised him that he would see the Savior before he died. On this day, the Holy Ghost told him the Savior was there. Simeon took the baby Jesus in his arms, and knew this little child would become the Savior of the World.

While holding Jesus, Simeon thanked Heavenly Father for that special moment. He told Mary and Joseph what a special child they had. Simeon knew that when Jesus grew up, he would teach wonderful things and redeem us from our sins.

Jesus was doing Heavenly Father's work

When Jesus was twelve years old, his family traveled to Jerusalem for a celebration. When the celebration was over, Mary and Joseph began traveling home, thinking Jesus was with them. But they soon discovered Jesus was not among the other children. They hurried back to Jerusalem and after three days they found him in the temple, talking with the city's religious leaders. These men were amazed at how smart Jesus was, because he knew more about the scriptures than they did.

When Mary found Jesus, she told him that she had been very worried about him. But he told her not to worry. He said he had been doing Heavenly Father's business. Even at that young age, Jesus knew he was sent to earth to do Heavenly Father's work.

Scripture:

And his mother said unto him, Son why hast thou thus dealt with us? Behold, thy father and I have sought thee sorrowing. And he said unto them, How is it that ye sought me? wist ye not that I must be about my Father's business?
(Luke 2: 48-49)

Visual Aid:
GAPK #205
Young Jesus in the Temple

Temples are now in many countries

Scripture:

And many nations shall come, and say, Come, and let us go up to the mountain of the Lord . . . and he will teach us of his ways, and we will walk in his paths.
(Micah 4:2)

Visual Aid:
GAPK #608
Jesus surrounded by modern children from many nations

We live in a time that is known as the last days before the Savior's Second Coming. For many centuries prophets have seen the last days in vision, and they knew it would be a time when temple work would be performed.

The best-known temple is the Salt Lake Temple. It is a symbol of our church, and people from many nations have come to do temple work there. But President Gordon B. Hinckley has announced a plan for smaller temples that will be built all over the world. More than 100 temples have been built, and more are dedicated every year. This means that families don't have to travel so far to receive temple blessings.

Many new temples are now open in countries that never had them before, and children from nearly every nation can now go to a temple and be sealed to their families for eternity. These new temples are a blessing from Heavenly Father.

Tithing money helps build temples

Heavenly Father has a wonderful way to pay for new temples. It is through tithing. Tithing is ten percent of what we earn. If you earn a dollar, you should pay ten cents of that as tithing. When we pay our tithing, part of that money will go toward building new temples. Sometimes church members in other countries don't have enough money to build temples or church meetinghouses, but when we pay our tithing, the church is able to build new buildings for them.

Heavenly Father is always happy when we pay our tithing. He has given us everything, even the world we live on. When we pay our tithing it shows him that we love him and want to obey his commandments.

Scripture:

Behold, this is the tithing and the sacrifice which I, the Lord, require at their hands, that there may be a house built unto me for the salvation of Zion.
(D&C 97:12)

Visual Aid:
GAPK #600
A view of Earth from Space

41

Chapter 8

We serve others through temple work

America's founders wanted their temple work done

Scripture:

And he shall turn the heart of the fathers to the children, and the heart of the children to their fathers.
(Malachi 4:6)

The Lord has said that the men who helped start the United States of America were some of the finest people who ever lived. But most of them had died before Joseph Smith restored the true church. However, once the St. George Temple was built, Heavenly Father allowed these righteous spirits to visit President Wilford Woodruff in the temple. Men such as George Washington and Thomas Jefferson told President Woodruff they wanted their temple work done.

President Woodruff spent the next few days doing the temple work for the fifty men who signed the Declaration of Independence, and also for fifty other men, such as Columbus and early presidents of the United States. President Woodruff said it was a great honor to do their temple work for them.[10]

Visual Aid:
GAPK #504
Wilford Woodruff

Today's Primary children were faithful spirits

Heavenly Father saved many of his strongest, most faithful spirits to come to earth in the latter days and be leaders in the church. President Joseph F. Smith saw a vision of these spirits, and he saw that temple work would be one of the most important things they would do while on the earth.

President Gordon B. Hinckley has said the young people in the church are also part of that faithful group. The Primary children of today will grow up, serve missions, raise righteous families, and help spread the gospel to all the world. We will also help build more temples throughout the world, and complete the temple work for our ancestors.

Scripture:

The Prophet Joseph Smith, and my father Hyrum Smith, Brigham Young, John Taylor, Wilford Woodruff, and other choice spirits who were reserved to ... take part in laying the foundations of the great latter-day work. Including the building of the temples and the performances of ordinances therein for the redemption of the dead.
(D&C 138:53-54)

Visual Aid:
GAPK #520
Gordon B. Hinckley

A vision of the Spirit World

Scripture:

The Prophet Elijah was to plant in the hearts of the children the promises made to the fathers. Foreshadowing the great work to be done in the temples of the Lord in the dispensation of the fulness of times, for the redemption of the dead, and the sealing of the children to their parents.
(D&C 138:47-48)

Visual Aid:
GAPK #511
Joseph F. Smith

In the year 1918, Joseph F. Smith was the prophet. In General Conference he told the church members that he had recently received several revelations from Heavenly Father. One of these revelations was a vision of the Savior's visit to the Spirit World after the crucifixion, while Jesus' body was in the tomb. President Smith saw Jesus teaching and preparing the faithful spirits such as Adam and Noah to be missionaries there, so they could teach the spirits who had never heard the gospel while they were alive.

Jesus knew that someday temple work could be done for these spirits, and they could live with Heavenly Father if they accepted the gospel. President Smith's vision is now recorded in Section 138 in the Doctrine and Covenants.

The prophets ask us to keep a journal

Heavenly Father has always asked his children to keep records of their lives. Even Adam and Eve recorded their life history. Prophets have always written down important events. The scriptures are a part of those records. For example, Mormon wrote on gold plates that became the Book of Mormon.

Our church keeps careful track of many records, but especially of temple work that is done. When a person's temple work is completed, it is recorded in a computer and placed in the church records.

Our church leaders today have asked us to keep a journal and write down important dates, such as our birthday and baptismal date. This is how our children and grandchildren will have records of our lives and know about special events that happened to us.

Scripture:

I have received a commandment of the Lord that I should make these plates, for the special purpose that there should be an account engraven of the ministry of my people. (1 Nephi 9:3)

Visual Aids:
GAPK #101
Adam and Eve

GAPK #306
Mormon writing on gold plates

Chapter 9

I prepare to go to the temple by following Heavenly Father's plan

The School of the Prophets

Scripture:

Establish a house, even a house of prayer, a house of fasting, a house of faith, a house of learning, a house of glory, a house of order, a house of God.
(D&C 88:119)

Visual Aid:
GAPK #400
Joseph Smith

When the gospel was first restored, the church members didn't always understand many of the gospel teachings. The Lord told Joseph Smith to build the Kirtland Temple as a place to teach the members sacred things. But Joseph needed to teach the members about the gospel before the temple could be built. He decided to organize a school for priesthood holders called the School of the Prophets.

Joseph taught them many lessons about prayer, fasting, and faith. As the men followed these gospel teachings, their testimonies grew stronger and many of them were called to serve missions for the church. Today we no longer have the School of the Prophets, but we can learn the same things Joseph taught the early Saints by going to church and then attending the temple when we are older.

We must be worthy to enter the temple

The temple is a sacred, holy place. People who want to enter the temple make a promise to obey the commandments. If you are worthy, the bishop gives you a card called a temple recommend. Once in a while a person might try to enter the temple unworthily, and sometimes the Holy Ghost tells a church leader when there is an unworthy person in the temple.

President John Taylor once saw a woman enter the Logan Temple. President Taylor didn't know the woman, but he told the temple president, "Don't let her in. The Spirit of God told me she is not worthy."

The temple president stopped the woman, and she admitted that she wasn't worthy. She had paid a friend for the recommend. This was not right, and the Holy Ghost helped the prophet know it.[11]

Scripture:

He that hath my commandments, and keepeth them, he it is that loveth me.
(John 14:21)

Visual Aids:
GAPK #611
The Bishop

GAPK # 503
John Taylor

Little children are learning the gospel

Scripture:

And ye will not suffer your children that they go hungry . . . Or transgress the laws of God. But ye will teach them to walk in the ways of truth and soberness; ye will teach them to love one another and serve one another.
(Mosiah 4:14-15)

Visual Aids:
GAPK #307
King Benjamin

GAPK #612
Missionaries visiting a family

The righteous prophets and kings in the Book of Mormon truly loved little children. They did their best to make sure they each had enough food and clothing. They also made sure the children were taught the gospel and learned Heavenly Father's commandments. King Benjamin taught his people to love and serve one another.

That is happening today all over the world. Missionaries are taking the gospel plan to many nations where the church has never been before, such as countries in Africa and South America. Many of the children there don't know the truth, but the missionaries teach them, and the children share the gospel plan with their family and friends. Someday there will be enough members in these areas to build a temple. Then these children can be sealed to their families forever.

The Savior visited the Nephite temple

When Jesus was crucified in Jerusalem, there was great destruction on the American continent. There were earthquakes and floods. The wicked Lamanites and Nephites were killed. It was dark for three days. When the sun finally came out, the people who were still alive gathered together at their temple.

Then Jesus came to visit them. He had been resurrected, and was wearing a white robe. He showed the people the nail prints in his hands and feet. He taught them the gospel and told them to be kind to each other. He also taught them about the sacrament. Jesus then selected twelve disciples to lead the church. After Jesus returned to heaven, the Nephite people were righteous for many years.

Scripture:

They saw a Man descending out of heaven; and he was clothed in a white robe; and he came down in the midst of them; . . . he stretched forth his hand and spake unto the people saying: Behold, I am Jesus Christ.
(3 Nephi 11:8-10)

Visual Aid:
GAPK #316
Jesus shows the Nephites the marks in his hands and feet

Chapter 10

I will live to be worthy and clean to go to the temple and serve a mission

The Articles of Faith

Scripture:

We believe that the first principles and ordinances of the Gospel are: first, Faith in the Lord Jesus Christ; second, Repentance; third, Baptism by immersion for the remission of sins; fourth, Laying on of hands for the gift of the Holy Ghost.
(Articles of Faith 1:4)

Visual Aids:
GAPK #601
A man being baptized

GAPK #602
A girl receiving the Holy Ghost

Joseph Smith was once asked by a newspaper editor from Chicago named John Wentworth to write a brief history of the church. Joseph did so, and at the end of the history he included what have become known as the Articles of Faith. They are thirteen statements that tell the world what we believe in. The fourth Article of Faith tells us what we need to do to become a member of the church.

First, we must have faith in Heavenly Father and Jesus. Second, we must do our best to keep the commandments, and repent if we do something wrong. When we are living righteously, we are ready to be baptized, which washes away our sins. Then a priesthood holder will confirm us a member of the church, and we receive the gift of the Holy Ghost. The Holy Ghost will guide us if we do what is right.

The gospel can bring peace

There once was a prophet named Alma in the Book of Mormon who lived during a time when the Nephites and the Lamanites were always fighting. Many people were killed, and many cities were destroyed. Alma and his friends, the sons of King Mosiah, decided to try something different. They went on missions among the wicked people to teach them the gospel plan.

After many years, their plan worked. The sons of Mosiah worked hard and were blessed during their missions among the Lamanites. They baptized many Lamanites, and the people they baptized became more righteous than the Nephites. There was peace in the land, because the Lamanites no longer wanted to fight. They wanted to obey Heavenly Father.

Scripture:

Preach unto them repentance, and faith on the Lord Jesus Christ; teach them to humble themselves and to be meek and lowly in heart; teach them to withstand every temptation of the devil, with their faith on the Lord Jesus Christ.
(Alma 37:33)

Visual Aid:
GAPK #311
Righteous Lamanites burying their swords

Even Jesus was baptized

For the gate by which ye should enter is repentance and baptism by water; and then cometh a remission of your sins by fire and by the Holy Ghost.
(2 Nephi 31:17)

Visual Aid:
GAPK # 208
Jesus being baptized

Baptism is the gateway to enter the Celestial Kingdom. A person must be baptized to join the Church of Jesus Christ. Jesus was baptized, even though he was sinless. He wanted to show us by example what we should do, so he went to the River Jordan and found John the Baptist. John had the priesthood authority to perform baptisms. He and Jesus went out into the water, and after saying the baptismal prayer, John put Jesus under the water, then pulled him back up.

Heavenly Father has made it possible for people who died without hearing the gospel to still become members of the church. If someone on earth goes to a temple and is baptized for someone who died, then that person is allowed to join the church in the Spirit World. It is a wonderful plan that will let us be reunited with our ancestors in the next life.

Missionaries are Heavenly Father's servants

Serving a mission is a wonderful way to show Heavenly Father that you are willing to obey his commandments. The prophet has said that every worthy young man in the church should serve a mission when he turns nineteen years old. Worthy young women who are at least twenty-one years old and not married are also invited to serve missions.

New missionaries go to a missionary training center for a few weeks. This is where they learn more about the gospel and also learn a language if they are going to another country. During their training, they go to the temple each week and feel closer to Heavenly Father. While in the temple we learn about Heavenly Father's plan and how to better follow his commandments.

Scripture:

But behold, I say unto you that ye must pray always, and not faint; that ye must not perform any thing unto the Lord save in the first place ye shall pray unto the Father in the name of Christ, that he will consecrate thy performance unto thee, that thy performance may be for the welfare of thy soul. (2 Nephi 32:9)

Visual Aid:
GAPK #612
Missionaries visiting a family

Chapter 11

I am thankful for temple blessings

Temples are dedicated by the Lord's servants

Scripture:

Let the hearts of all my people rejoice, who have, with their might, built this house to my name.
(D&C 110:6)

When a new temple is completed, the church holds what is called an open house for a few weeks before the temple is dedicated. During this time, people who aren't members of the church are able to take tours of the temple and see the beautiful rooms. Most people who live near a new temple are often curious about it, and on the tour they learn what happens in the temple. Many times the people are so impressed that they want to learn more about the church.

Then the temple is ready to be dedicated in a special ceremony. During this ceremony President Hinckley or one of the Twelve Apostles gives a special prayer dedicating the temple to Heavenly Father. After the dedication, only church members who are worthy are allowed to enter the temple, because it is a sacred place.

Visual Aids:
GAPK #505
Washington D.C. Temple

GAPK #520
Gordon B. Hinckley

We want to live in the Celestial Kingdom

In Heavenly Father's plan of salvation, there are three kingdoms of glory that people will be assigned after they are resurrected. The highest kingdom is the Celestial Kingdom. That is where Heavenly Father and Jesus live. Families that are sealed in the temple and live righteously will be able to live there, too.

People who were good citizens and neighbors but who didn't follow Heavenly Father's commandments will live in the Terrestrial Kingdom. It will be nice there, but it will also be sad, because they won't live with Heavenly Father.

The Telestial Kingdom is for people who committed very serious sins. They disobeyed Heavenly Father and broke most of the commandments. The people who live there will know they could have done better. Our goal should be to live righteously, so we can live again with Heavenly Father and Jesus.

Scripture:

But learn that he who doeth the works of righteousness shall receive his reward, even peace in this world, and eternal life in the world to come.
(D&C 59:23)

Visual Aid:
GAPK #239
Picture of Resurrected Jesus

Scripture:

And ye cannot bear all things now; nevertheless, be of good cheer, for I will lead you along. The kingdom is yours and the blessings thereof are yours, and the riches of eternity are yours.
(D&C 78:18)

Visual Aid:
GAPK #511
Joseph F. Smith

We are sent to earth to learn how to become better people, so that someday we can become like Heavenly Father and Jesus. But sometimes we have experiences that are hard. Sometimes we have trouble in school, or someone we love dies. These challenges aren't easy, but Heavenly Father promises that if we stay cheerful and keep the commandments during hard times, we will live with him forever.

Joseph F. Smith faced many challenges. When he was just a boy, his father Hyrum was killed in Carthage Jail. His family was forced to leave Nauvoo and cross the plains in a wagon. Then at age 15 he was called to serve a mission in Hawaii. He had to live in a wet, muddy shack. But he did his best all his life, and he was blessed. He later became the sixth president of the church.

Jesus blessed the little children

When Jesus visited the Nephites at their temple, he taught them many gospel teachings. He loved the people, and healed all the people that were sick.

Then he asked all the little children to be brought to him. The children sat on the ground around him, and Jesus asked their parents to kneel down. Then Jesus gave a special prayer, asking Heavenly Father to bless the people. After the prayer, Jesus blessed each of the children.

Then a wonderful event took place. Angels appeared from heaven, and they surrounded the children. These angels were so glorious that it looked like the children were surrounded by fire. But this wasn't scary to the children or their parents who were watching, because they knew the angels had been sent by Heavenly Father.

Scripture:

They saw the heavens open, and they saw angels descending out of heaven as if it were in the midst of fire, and they came down and encircled those little ones about, and they were encircled with fire; and the angels did minister unto them.
(3 Nephi 17: 24)

Visual Aids:
GAPK #317
Jesus blesses Nephite children

GAPK # 322
Angels surrounding Nephite children

Chapter 12

When Jesus comes again, He will come to the temple

Everyone will know when Jesus returns

Scripture:

And if you are faithful, behold, I am with you until I come. And verily, verily, I say unto you, I come quickly. I am your Lord and your Redeemer. (D&C 34:11-12)

Visual Aids:
GAPK #200
Baby Jesus in a stable

GAPK # 238
The Savior's Second Coming

When Jesus was a boy, he lived a normal life with his family. Only a few people knew him. He grew up near Jerusalem, which is usually a dry, dusty place. So even though Jesus was the Son of God, he would sometimes get tired, hungry and thirsty, just like we do.

But now Jesus is a resurrected person. When the Savior returns to earth at his Second Coming, it will be much different than when he came the first time. This time, everyone on earth will know that the Savior has returned. The wicked will be destroyed, and the Millennium will begin. Jesus will then visit his followers at the temples they have built. When the Savior is on the earth, the temple will be his home.

The Saints will build New Jerusalem

Many great events still await the members of the church. One of the most glorious promises in the scriptures is that the church members will someday build a wonderful city called New Jerusalem. This city will be built in the state of Missouri. The most important building in this new city will be a large, beautiful temple. New Jerusalem will be built just before the Second Coming of the Savior.

When Jesus comes again, the wicked people will be destroyed and Jesus will personally lead the church. The earth will be renewed as it was when the Garden of Eden was on the earth. All animals will be friendly to each other. Beautiful plants and trees will grow everywhere, and there will be peace on earth. The period of time after Jesus returns will be called the Millennium and will last one thousand years.

Scripture:

We believe in the literal gathering of Israel and in the restoration of the Ten Tribes; that Zion (the New Jerusalem) will be built upon the American continent; that Christ shall reign personally upon the earth; and, that the earth will be renewed and receive its paradisiacal glory.
(Articles of Faith 1:10)

Visual Aid:
GAPK #100
The Creation (used to show conditions during Millennium)

Jesus will come in the clouds of heaven

Scripture:

And then they shall look for me, and, behold, I will come; and they shall see me in the clouds of heaven, clothed with power and great glory; with all the holy angels; and he that watches not for me shall be cut off.
(D&C 45:44)

The scriptures teach us that the time is soon when Jesus will come again. All wars will stop, and peace will come to the earth.

When the Savior returns, he will come in the sky, with thousands of angels at his side. Everyone on earth will recognize his power and glory. This will be the beginning of the Millennium.

One of the most important things that will be done during the Millennium is temple work. Thousands of temples will be built, and the church members living on the earth will do the baptisms and temple ordinances for those who died without the gospel, but who accepted it in the spirit world. It will be a glorious time.

Visual Aid:
GAPK # 238
The Savior's Second Coming

The righteous will wear white robes

John was one of the Savior's apostles, and he was given a vision that is now found in the Bible. John saw people wearing white robes, and he asked who they were. He was told that they are the church members who follow Jesus and attend the temple.

When we go to the temple we wear white clothing. This helps us remember that only those people who have repented of their sins and are pure can enter Heavenly Father's kingdom.

To travel to another country, we need to have a passport. In a similar way, the temple ordinances are like a passport to the Celestial Kingdom. If we attend the temple, learn the gospel plan, and keep the commandments, we will be able to live with Heavenly Father and Jesus forever.

Scripture:

And one of the elders answered, saying unto me, What are these which are arrayed in white robes? And whence came they? . . . And he said unto me, These are they which came out of great tribulation, and have washed their robes, and made them white in the blood of the Lamb. Therefore are they before the throne of God, and serve him day and night in his temple.
(Revelation 7:13-15)

Visual Aid:
GAPK #240
The Resurrected Savior

References

1 *Autobiography of Truman O. Angell*, p. 4-5.

2 *Ensign*, May 1974, p. 58.

3 Doctrine and Covenants 137:1-8.

4 *Deseret News*, Church Section, April 2, 1938, p.3.

5 *Deseret News*, Church Section, Dec. 12, 1936, p. 2.

6 Documentary History of the Church, 6:196-197.

7 *Ensign*, Nov. 1997, p. 49.

8 *The Life of Jonathan Hale*, p. 170-171.

9 Letter written by David Henry Cannon, Jr., contained in *History of the St. George Temple*, Kirk M. Curtis, p. 24-25.

10 Journal of Discourses 19:229.

11 N.B. Lundwall, *Temples of the Most High*, p. 104-105.

Watch for upcoming
volumes in the
Tiny Talks series:

Volume 2:
The Savior

Volume 3:
Latter-day Prophets

About the authors

Tammy and Chad Daybell live in Springville, Utah, with their five children.

Tammy Douglas Daybell was born in California and moved to Springville as a teenager. She served as Springville High's yearbook editor and played the drums in the marching band. She attended BYU as an advertising major. Her kids keep her pretty busy, but in her spare time she enjoys reading, gardening, and designing websites.

Chad Daybell was born in Provo, Utah, and was raised in Springville. He served an LDS mission among the Spanish-speaking people in northern New Jersey.

In 1992 he graduated from BYU with a bachelor's degree in journalism, where he served as the City Editor of *The Daily Universe*. Later, he worked for several years as a newspaper editor at *The Standard-Examiner* in Ogden, Utah.

Chad has also written the award-winning LDS series ***The Emma Trilogy***.

The trilogy's novels—***An Errand for Emma***, ***Doug's Dilemma***, and ***Escape to Zion***—are exciting adventures written for teenagers and adults that teach the three missions of the church. Through the time-travel experiences of the Daltons, a modern-day LDS family, readers first step back into the past with Brigham Young, then later view the church's future in New Jerusalem.

Visit **www.cdaybell.com** to learn more about the authors and these LDS titles.

About the illustrator

Adam Ford graduated from BYU with an emphasis in Illustration Design.

He grew up in San Jose, California, and served an LDS mission in South Korea. He and his wife Amanda live in Provo, Utah.

CEDAR FORT, INCORPORATED
Order Form

Name:_____

Address: _____

City: _____ State: _____ Zip: _____

Phone: (   ) _____ Daytime phone: (   ) _____

Tiny Talks: Volume 1—Temples

Quantity: _____ @ $7.95 each: _____

plus $3.49 shipping & handling for the first book: _____

(add 99¢ shipping for each additional book)

Utah residents add 6.25% for state sales tax: _____

                                        TOTAL: _____

Please make check or money order payable to:
Cedar Fort, Incorporated.

Mail this form and payment to:
Cedar Fort, Inc.
925 North Main St.
Springville, UT 84663

9 ‖26575 76127‖ 9

You can also order on our website **www.cedarfort.com**
or e-mail us at sales@cedarfort.com or call 1-800-SKYBOOK